How to Reach Taj Mahal

The Taj Mahal is a symbol of love and romance. It can be found in Agra, which lies about 204km south of Delhi. The monument is a UNESCO World Heritage Site, and one of the Seven Wonders of the World. It attracts hordes of tourists from around the world.

The world, year-round. The monument's charismatic appeal and magnetic attraction is so strong that people can't get enough and want to return time after time. If you are captivated by this magnificent monument's architectural beauty and plan to visit it, the first question that will come to mind is how to get there. This section will discuss the various routes to reach the Taj Mahal in India.

By Air

Flying is the fastest way to reach Taj Mahal, Agra. Agra's airport is located approximately 7km from the center of the city. Indian Airlines operates daily flights to Agra.

By Rail

Agra is connected to the rest of India by a network of trains. There are two other stations, Raja-ki-Mandi (the main railway station in Agra Cantonment) and Agra Fort (the second station). Palace on Wheels and Rajdhani are the main trains linking Agra to Delhi.

By Road

Regular bus services run from Agra to many important cities. There are buses that run to Delhi, Jaipur and Mathura from the main bus station at Idgah.

Local Transportation

To reach Taj Mahal, you will need some form of transport once you have reached the city. There are many options for transportation in the city, including taxi, tempo and auto-rickshaw. If you wish to explore the many places in the vicinity, prepaid taxis can be arranged. You can rent bicycles on an hourly basis in different areas of the city for the more adventurous. You can find electric buses, horse-driven tongas and other pollution-free vehicles in the vicinity.

Best Time to Visit Taj Mahal

The best time to visit: October-March

There is no "bad time" to visit the Taj Mahal, just as there is no "bad time" to live. The Taj Mahal will continue its mission to spread its charm, glory and shine no matter what season it is. The heat can be unbearable for those who visit the Taj Mahal in summer months. Therefore, it is recommended to avoid the warmer months (i.e. The best time to visit Taj Mahal is usually October to March. The beauty of the Taj Mahal's radiance is simply stunning. It changes with each hour and reflects a different aura during different seasons. The Taj Mahal's visual beauty is best at sunset and sunrise.

Taj Mahal at Sunrise

It is amazing to see the sun rise from the sea of clouds. You can witness it while standing on the grounds of one of the Seven Wonders of the World. The combination of the beauty of sunrise and Taj Mahal creates an amazing moment of delight.

Taj Mahal at Sunset

After shining its glory throughout the day, the sun descends the stairway to heavens and prepares to bid farewell to the world. The final trick it does is to lend Taj Mahal a new appearance. It transforms the fiery yellow into an exotic orange, and then back to pearl white, until the full Moon returns to join the Taj, dazzling the entire world with its peaceful heavenly elegance.

Taj Mahal under Full Moon Night

The beauty of Taj Mahal's night sky is so beautiful that it is difficult to describe. The silver glow that surrounds Taj Mahal is so captivating that almost all other things will seem ordinary after it. The amazing interplay of colors throughout the day and night symbolises the presence of God. He is not represented in anthropomorphic form.

It is best to arrive just before sunrise or sunset. Night viewing is permitted on full moon nights, two days prior and two days following it. You must book tickets for the same at least one day in advance.

Taj Mahal Timings

Timings: Sunrise to Sunset, Every Day (except Friday).

Night, 8:30 PM to 12:30AM (On Full moon night two days prior and two days thereafter)

Day Fee: Rs 1100 (Foreigners)

Rs 540 (Citizens in SAARC and BIMSTEC countries)

Indian / OCI Cardholders: Rs 50

Children under 15 years old are eligible for free entry

Note: Rs. Note: Rs.

Night Fee: Rs 750 (Adult, Foreign)

Rs 510 (Adult, Indian)
Rs 500 (Child between 3 and 15 Years, Indian & Other)

Children under 3 years old are not allowed to enter

The Archeological Survey of India determines the timings for visiting the Taj Mahal. The Taj Mahal is open every day except Fridays. This is for people who need to pray at the Taj Mosque. The hours are from sunrise to sunset. Tickets can be purchased at both the eastern and western gates. At the southern gate, tickets are available between 8:00 AM and 5:00 PM. Tourists can spend as many hours as they like in the Taj complex, from sunrise to sunset.

The Taj Mahal is open nightly from 8:30 PM to 12:30 am. Fridays are excluded. Night viewing is restricted to 400 people per night. Each batch can visit the Taj Mahal for 30 minutes. Tickets for night viewing must be reserved one day in advance (24 hours), at the booking counter in the Archeological Survey of India Agra Circle 22 The Mall, Agra. Uttar Pradesh, between 10:00 AM and 6:00 PM.

Taj Mahal Location
City: Agra on the banks river Yamuna

State: Uttar Pradesh
Distance from Delhi: 204 km (approx).

The city of Agra has been honored with the Seven Wonders of the World title, the Taj Mahal, which is a place for eternal love in its courtyard. Agra, located in India's northern state of Uttar Pradesh is a powerful city that has existed since medieval times. It is mentioned in the epic Mahabharata. Later, it was recognized as the capital city of the Mughal Empire, which lasted from 1526 to 1658, under Shah Jahan, Jahangir and Akbar. The city of Agra was known at that time as Akbarabad. It is still a popular tourist destination thanks to three iconic Mughal era buildings, including Agra Fort and Fatehpur Sikri. But the most notable of these three buildings, the magnificent Taj Mahal, are all listed as UNESCO World Heritage Sites. One of the most well-known buildings in the world is the Taj Mahal. It was built by Shah Jahan to honor his beloved wife Mumtaz Mahal. Millions of tourists visit it annually.

Shah Jahan made a thoughtful decision to locate Taj Mahal at a quiet spot about one-and-a-half miles from Agra, on the south bank of river Yamuna. The emperor also found this location strategic because it could be seen from the Agra Fort palace. This location's proximity to the Yamuna River gave it a scenic edge and also allowed for the provision of water during construction and the laying out of the garden. The Taj complex is made up of several buildings, including a mausoleum and a guesthouse. It also houses Shah Jahan and Mumtaz Mahal's tombs. The main mausoleum is reached via a long, beautiful walkway made of pure white marble. The gardens in front of the Taj are divided into four sections by four waterways. They then meet at the center in a pool. This strategic location is thought to be responsible for half the beauty of Taj Mahal.

It's easy to get to the Taj Mahal and the magnificent Taj Mahal from Agra, due to its location in the Agra city. You can reach the Taj Mahal within 6km of

Agra's city centre by taxi or auto rickshaw. It is easily accessible by road from all major Indian cities, thanks to its excellent connectivity via national highways. Agra Cantt, Agra Fort Railway Station (from which the Taj is located at 1015m walking distance), Raja ki Mandi and Agra Cantt are the three railway stations that connect nearly all major cities in India and allow easy access to the Taj. Flying to Agra is the best way to get to the Taj Mahal if you are very busy and still want to enjoy the beautiful city. Indian Airways has flights arriving and departing daily from Agra Airport, located approximately 6 kilometers from the city center.

Attractions Near Taj Mahal

Agra was the capital of Mughal Empire and witnessed many buildings being built on a large scale. Agra has many monuments and other places that are worthy of being visited, aside from the Taj Mahal. If you're planning on visiting Agra next time you go on holiday, make sure to take a few days to explore the city beyond the magnificent Taj Mahal. These places should be included in your itinerary so that you can immerse yourself in the Mughal epical era. Below is more information about the most popular attractions around Taj Mahal in Agra.

Tourist Attractions Near Taj Mahal

Agra Fort

The Agra Fort, India's most famous tourist spot, is located near Taj Mahal.

It is located near Taj Mahal and was built by Emperor Akbar in 1565. This fort was home to many additions, which continued until Shah Jahan's time.

It is a beautiful example of Mughal architecture, entirely made of red sandstone. It is also UNESCO World Heritage Site.

Akbar's Tomb, Sikandra

The tomb of Akbar is located at Sikandra and is just 13 km from Agra Fort. This tomb's architectural style is very different from most of the Mughal tombs. Jahangir, Akbar's son, completed this pyramidal tomb in 1613. It has the 99 names Allah inscribed on its surface.

Fatehpur Sikri

Near Agra is the deserted city Fatehpur Sikri. It was built by Mughal Emperor Akbar and completed in 1584. It is located 35 km from Agra and is considered one of the most magnificent cities in the Mughal Empire. It is also one of three UNESCO World Heritage Sites located in Agra. The other two are Taj Mahal or Agra Fort.

Itmad-ud-Daulah Tomb

Noor Jahan, Jahangir's wife, got the Itmad ud-Daulah's tomb built in 1622-1628 AD. It was built in memory of her father Ghiyasud-Din Beg. The tomb, which is located on the left bank river Yamuna is an elegant structure that is considered an antecedent to the Taj Mahal due to its intricate carvings.

Mankameshwar Temple

One of the four temples dedicated to Lord Shiva, located at each corner of Agra city, is situated 2.5km from Taj Mahal. It is surrounded with the markets from the Mughal era.

Ram Bagh

Ram Bagh, which was built by Babur in 1528 is India's oldest Mughal garden. It is located on the Yamuna River, just 3 km from Taj Mahal. The garden was designed to allow the river's wind and greenery to cool the area during peak summer days. This garden was originally called Aram Bagh, or the Garden of Relaxation.

Swami Bagh Samadhi

Swami Bagh Samadhi was built more than 100 years ago in 1904. Construction continues to this day. Because of its unique combination of marbles, carvings in stone and colorful marbles, it is often called the next Taj Mahal. It holds the ashes and Sri Shiv Dayal Seth's Huzur Swamiji Maharaj.

Vrindavan

Vrindavan is a holy city near Agra that is revered by Hindus. It is closely associated with Lord Krishna. There are reportedly 4,000 temples dedicated to Him.

Other Attractions

Jama Masjid was built for Shah Jahan's daughters; Guru ka Tal is a holy place for Sikhs to worship; Chini Ka Rauza is dedicated to Shah Jahan Prime Minister; Mariam's Tomb; Mehtab Bagh is a moonlit garden; Keetham Lake are other nearby attractions.

Shah Jahan

January 5, 1592 - Born

December 22, 1666, Died

Achievements: The founder of the majestic monument Taj Mahal. Also associated with Jama Masjid, Delhi, Section of Agra Fort and Wazir Khan Mosque, as well as the Red Fort of Delhi, Jama Masjid, Delhi, Section of Agra Fort and the Moti Masjid, Lahore in Pakistan.

Shah Jahan was the Mughal Emperor of Southern Asia, his name and that of his wife Mumtaz Mahal being synonymous with Taj Mahal's existence and growing popularity. He ruled from 1627-1658. Shah Jahan, the son of Emperor Jahangir, was born as Prince Shihab-ud-din Muhammad Khurram, Lahore in Pakistan. His grandfather Akbar the great gave him the name Khurram which means "joyful" and was a Persian translation of his Persian name. His father was impressed by his military skills and his ability to defeat many enemies, including Mewar, the Lodi of the Deccan, Kangra, and Kangra. Shah Jahan Bahadur received the title Shah Jahan Bahadur. He was not only a skilled military leader but also had an extraordinary talent for building. This was proven by his re-designing of buildings in the Agra fort. He was a multi-talented man, but "The Builder of the Marvels", one of his many titles was soon to be proclaimed the best.

Shah Jahan's most important part of his life began in 1607, when he was 15. He was only 14 years old at the time and was engaged to Arjumand Banu Begum, the daughter of a Persian noble. Arjumand was the undisputed love of his life after they were married in 1612. Khurram awarded her the title Mumtaz Mahal meaning "Jewel of the Palace", after he saw her character and appearance.

Mumtaz was one of the few wives Shah Jahan had. However, Qazwini, an official court chronicler, stated that the relationship with Shah Jahan's other wives was "only the status of marriage." His Majesty's deep love, affection and favor for the Cradle of Excellence, Mumtaz, was more than he had for any other woman. He considered her his constant companion and trusted confidante.

Shah Jahan, who had just given birth to their 14th child in 1631, took on the task of building the world's most magnificent monument in her honor. The monument, which includes Shah Jahan and Mumtaz Mahal, was built over 22 years. It took 22000 workers to build. Shah Jahan died in 1657. Dara, Mumtaz Mahal's oldest son, assumed the throne. Aurangzeb, his other son, marched to Agra with his younger brothers Shuja, Murad, to claim their share. They defeated Dara's army and declared Shah Jahan incompetent. Two men took Shah Jahan's body and placed it beside Mumtaz after he died in captivity in 1666. The Taj Mahal, one of the Seven Wonders of the World and the Red Fort of Delhi, Jama Masjid of Delhi Section of Agra Fort, the Wazir Khan Mosque, the Wazir Khan Mosque, the Moti Masjid, Lahore, Pakistan are just a few of the magnificent structures that were associated with Shah Jahan's name, which means "King of the World" to Persian.

Mumtaz Mahal

Born On: April, 1593
Born In: Agra
Died On: June 17, 1631

Shah Jahan, who created the Taj Mahal in love, beauty and dedication to Mumtaz Maul, fulfilled his long-held desire to immortalize Mumtaz Mahal's name. Mumtaz Mahal is so revered that everyone who has ever heard of Taj Mahal knows her. She was born Arjumand Banu Beum in 1593. She was the daughter and princess of the Persian nobility. Her beauty was so captivating that Shah Jahan (then Prince) chose to marry her.

Khurram) fell in love at first sight with her. In 1607, she was married to Prince Khurram. She quickly became the undisputed love of her life. Their marriage was formalized five years later, in 1612. This began one of the most famous love stories in the world. She was Shah Jahan's favorite wife, even though she was one of his three wives. He gave her the name Mumtaz Mahal, which means "Jewel of the Palace", as well as the highest honor in the land, Mehr Uzaz.

Mumtaz Mahal was a deeply loving wife to Shah Jahan. Poets would praise her beauty, grace, and compassion even during her lifetime. She was his trusted companion, and travelled with him throughout the Mughal Empire. Mumtaz was only one of three wives Shah Jahan had, the other two being Akbarabadi Mahal or Kandahari Mahal. According to Qazwini, his relationship with the other wives was "no more than a marriage status." His Majesty's deep love, affection and favor for Mumtaz (the Cradle of Excellence) was more than he had for any other woman. She was a perfect wife, and it is believed she had no ambitions to be a politician. She was a loving wife to Emperor Shah Jahan and a counselor.

Mumtaz Mahal was with Shah Jahan in 1630, as he was fighting in the Deccan Plateau. She didn't know it was her last journey. In 1631, Mumtaz Mahal died while giving birth to their 14th child and fled for the holy abode. Shah Jahan is said to have been so devastated by the devastation, that he was inconsolable. Burhanpur was the final resting place for her remains. Shah Jahan however, decided to create the world's most expensive mausoleum in his memory of Jewel. Mumtaz. To build a monument to his wife's memory, it took her husband 22 year and all of his royal treasury. The Taj Mahal, the most beautiful building in all of the universe, is now in Mumtaz Mahal's name. It is a monument to love, purity, and unsurpassed beauty.

History of Taj Mahal

For more than its stunning beauty, the Taj Mahal of Agra is one of the Seven Wonders of the World. The history of Taj Mahal adds an extra dimension to its beauty: it is a place that is full of love, loss and remorse. Without love, the world wouldn't have a good example to follow in their relationships. This is an example of how deeply a man loves his wife. He made sure that the memory would never be forgotten, even though she was only a memory. This was Shah Jahan, the Mughal Emperor Shah Jahan. He was madly in love with Mumtaz Mahal his beloved wife. He was the son and grandson of Akbar The Great, the Mughal Emperor Jehangir, and was a Muslim Persian princess. He met Mumtaz at 14 and fell in love. They were married five years later, in 1612.

Mumtaz Mahal was Shah Jahan's inseparable companion. She died while giving birth in 1631 to their 14th child. Shah Jahan, in memory of his beloved wife, built a beautiful monument to pay tribute to her. It is now known as the "Taj Mahal". In 1631, the construction of Taj Mahal began. It took 22 years to construct what we see today. The empire needed stonecutters, masons, inlayers and carvers as well as painters, calligraphers and domebuilders. It was a symbol of love and employed the services of over 22,000 workers and 1,000 elephants. It was entirely constructed of white marble imported from India and central Asia. Taj Mahal was completed in 1653 after a cost of 32 million rupees.

Shah Jahan was executed by his son Aurangzeb shortly after completion of Taj Mahal. He was placed under house arrest at Agra Fort. Shah Jahan and his wife are also buried in this mausoleum. Further back in history, the British Viceroy Lord Curzon, at the end 19th century, ordered a massive restoration project. This was to replace the damage done during the Indian rebellion. Taj was also damaged by British soldiers and officials, who also removed precious stones and lapis li from the walls. The British-style lawns, which add to the beauty and charm of Taj, were also remodeled at the same time. Despite the controversies and current threats from Indo-Pak war, environmental pollution, and other unforeseen controversies that surround it, this symbol of love continues to shine and attract people all over the globe.

Taj Mahal Story

Male Protagonist: Shah Jahan, Prince Khurram

Female Protagonist:Mumtaz Mahal, Arjumand Banu Begum

The magnificent Taj Mahal monument, which stands in the heart of India, has a story that has touched the hearts of millions since its creation. Although the story ended in 1631, it lives on today in Taj Mahal, which is considered an example of eternal love. It is the story of Shah Jahan's love for Mumtaz Mahal. These two individuals have set an example for people today and in the future. Sir Edwin Arnold, an English poet, best described it as "Not architecture as such, but the proud passions of an emperor's love wrought from living stones." The story below will show why this statement is true.

Shah Jahan was originally called Prince Khurram when he was born in 1592. He was the fourth Mughal emperor in India, Jehangir. Shah Jahan saw a girl selling silk and glass beads while he was walking down the Meena Bazaar in 1607. It was love at first glance. The girl was Mumtaz Mahal who was then known as Arjumand Barutum. He was only 14 years old at the time and she, a Muslim Persian princess was just 15. Shah Jahan met her and decided to marry her. After five years, i.e. in the year 1612, the marriage was legally consummated.

Shah Jahan, in 1628, was made Emperor and gave Arjumand Banu the royal seal. He also gave her the title of Mumtaz Mahal which means the "Jewel of the Palace". Although Shah Jahan had many wives, Mumtaz Mahal was his favourite and accompanied him everywhere. Mumtaz Mahal, who was about to give birth to their fourteenth child in 1631, died from complications. Mumtaz died in her bed, and Shah Jahan promised that he would never marry again and that he will build the most beautiful mausoleum for her.

According to legend, Shah Jahan was so devastated by her death that he ordered his court to mourn for two years. Shah Jahan, in memory of his beloved, began the work of building the most beautiful monument on the planet. The monument was built over 22 years with the help of 22,000 workers. Shah Jahan's death in 1666 saw his body placed in a grave next to Mumtaz Mahal. This incredible monument became known as "Taj Mahal", and is now one of the Seven Wonders of the World. This is the real story of India's Taj Mahal, which has captivated many with its stunning beauty.

Taj Mahal Facts

Are you planning a trip to the Taj Mahal. You may have a few questions about the Taj Mahal, such as who built it, what time is best to visit, how to pay, and other details that you would like to know before visiting. You don't have to worry about it, because this section on "Taj Mahal Facts" will give you a few quick facts and answer any basic questions you may have. Continue reading to learn more about Agra and Taj Mahal. Don't waste your time. You don't have to worry about packing your bags or finding tickets. This monument is the epitome of love at its best.

Fast Facts

Year of Construction: 1631
Completed In: 1653
Time Taken: 22 years
Built By: Shah Jahan
This tribute is to Mumtaz Mahal (Arjumand Bo Begum), Shah's wife

Jahan
Location: Agra (Uttar Pradesh), India

Building Type: Islamic tomb
Architecture: Mughal (Combination Persian, Islamic, and Indian architecture styles)

Architect: Ustad Ahmad Lahauri
Construction Cost: 32 Crores

Number of workers: 20,000
Highlights: One of the Seven Wonders of the World, A UNESCO World

Heritage Site
Timings Sunrise to Sunset (Friday closed).

Fee: Rs 750 (Foreign Tourists)

Rs 510 (Citizens in SAARC & BIMSTEC countries)

Domestic Indian Tourists: Rs 20

Children below 15 years old (domestic or foreigner) are eligible for free entry

Interesting Facts Of Taj Mahal

Shah Jahan, before his accession to power, was known popularly as Prince Khurram.

Shah Jahan fell for Arjumand Bano Beum, and he married her to make her his third wife.

Shah Jahan christened Arjumand Bano Begum Mumtaz Mahal. This means the "Chosen One Of The Palace" (or "Jewel of the Palace").

Shah Jahan lost Mumtaz Mahal when she gave birth to their 14th child. More than 1000 elephants were used to transport the construction materials.

For the Taj's exquisite inlay work, 28 types of semi-precious or precious stones were used.

Taj Mahal can appear to change in color depending on the time of day and whether there is a moon at night. Many believe this shifting pattern of colors is a sign of different moods in a woman.

The complex has decorative elements such as Quran passages.

99 names of Allah are found in calligraphic inscriptions on the sides of Mumtaz Mahal's actual tomb.

The Taj Mahal was constructed in stages. The plinth and tomb took approximately 15 years to complete. Additional 5 years were required to complete the construction of minarets and mosques, jawab and gateway.

Different types of marble used in Taj Mahal construction were imported from different countries and regions: India, Pakistan, China, Tibet. Afghanistan, Srilanka.

During the Indian rebellion of 1857, many precious stones and Lapis Lazuli (a half-precious gemstone) were taken from the walls of the British Embassy.

Taj Mahal Architecture

It was the culmination of 22,000 workers, including stonecutters and inlayers, carvers and painters. 22 years later, a monument that combines Persian, Islamic and Indian architectural styles became a magnificent sight. Its grandeur was so impressive that it is still one of the most striking and eye-catching man-made monuments in the world, even after decades. It is not just the Taj that adds beauty and artistic wonder to the area. The Taj complex is made up of five main components: Darwaza (main gateway), Bageecha, Masjid (mosque), Naqar Khana(rest house), and Rauza (main Mausoleum).

The Taj Mahal spans 42 acres. The terrain slopes from the south to the north towards the Yamuna through descending terraces. From 1932 to 1938, the main entrance, located at the end the long watercourse, is decorated with calligraphy and verses from Holy Quran. It also has a central chamber with a dome. Solid silver was used to make the original entrance to this huge sandstone gateway. The door was designed to prevent people from seeing the tomb, until they are inside the doorway. The main entrance to Taj Mahal is characterized by vertical symmetry and is bordered by Arabic calligraphy, which is made of blackstone, that contains verses from Quran.

To reduce river seepage, the main Taj Mahal tomb is situated on a rectangular platform raised 50 meters above the riverbank. To emphasize the dome's beautiful, spherical shape (58 feet in diameter, 81 feet high), the four minarets at each corner of this square have been left unattached. On the western side of the main shrine is the mosque, while the Naqqar Khana (rest/guesthouse) is on the eastern side. Both are made from red sandstone. These two structures provide an architectural symmetry and an aesthetic contrast. The mosque and rest house are a marvel, even though they are at opposite ends. They look almost identical.

The garden covers 300 meters by 300 meters of the 580 meter x 300 meter total area. This garden is a perfect example of the impeccable symmetry. This garden's Islamic-style architecture symbolizes spirituality. According to the Holy Quran the lush green well watered symbolises Paradise in Islam. Each quarter is divided into 16 flowerbeds, each with approximately 400 plants. The garden is still considered the best spot to take photos of the main tomb.

The Taj Mahal's shadowy burial crypt houses Mumtaz Mahal's and Shah Jahan's tombs. Shah Jahan was buried there shortly after his death. The main chamber has the false tombs. Perforated marble screens and light transmission devices have been installed to allow light to enter the chamber. This is typical of mausoleums built by the Mughals. Both tombs are inlaid with semi-precious stones. On the sides of Mumtaz Mahal's actual tomb, you will find calligraphic inscriptions describing the ninety-nine names of Allah. There are many wonderful examples of polychrome-inlay art in the Taj, both on the exterior and interior of the dados and on the cenotaphs. Shah Jahan's tomb is located next to Mumtaz Mahal's and disturbs the otherwise perfect symmetry. Taj Mahal Calligraphy

Every visitor to the Taj Mahal is welcomed with a beautiful handwritten inscription on the gate. It reads, "O Soul, thou art in rest." "Return to the Lord at Peace with Him, and He with you," was the inscription that Abdul Haq wrote in beautiful handwriting on the great gate. Emperor Shah Jahan bestowed the title of "Amanat Khan" upon him. The Taj Mahal's surface is decorated with exquisite architecture and beautiful backgrounds. The Taj Mahal's calligraphy mainly contains verses and passages taken from the Holy Book of Quran. The jasper was inlaid in the panels of white marble. These passages were written by Amanat Khan using an obscure Thuluth script. Some panels bear his signatures.

Black marble was used to decorate the south gateway as well as the main mausoleum, with Arabic inscriptions. These texts refer to the themes judgment and the fruitful, paradisiacal rewards that await the faithful. The gateway's inscriptions invite the reader into the paradise. As one approaches the main mausoleum the tone of the inscriptions shifts from paradisiacal into that of a coming doom for those who don't believe on the Day of Judgment. Once inside the mausoleum however, the tone of inscriptions shifts from judgement to paradisiacal. Amanat Khan may have chosen the passages to calligraphy Taj Mahal, Agra. You will find verses from Quran on the exterior of Taj Mahal:

Surah 91 (The Sun)
Surah 112 ("The Purity of Faith")

Surah 89 (Daybreak)
Surah 93 (Morning Light)

Surah 95 (The Fig)
Surah 94 (The Solace)
Surah 36 (Ya Sin)
Surah 81 (The folding up)

Surah 82 ("The Cleaving Asunder")

Surah 84 ("The Rending Asunder")

Surah 98 (The Evidence)
Surah 67 (Dominion)
Surah 48 (Victory)
Surah 77 (Those Sent Forth)

Surah 39 (The Crowds)

The actual Mumtaz Mahal tomb, which is located in the burial chamber's crypt, has ninety names for God as calligraphic inscriptions. These include "O Noble, Eternal, O Magnificent and O Unique", "O Noble, O Majificent, O Unique, O Eternal, O Glory " and "He traveled from this world to a banquet hall of eternal on the night of twenty sixth of the Month of Rajab in the year 1076 Hijri, in the 26 of the six of the twentieth of the [in the] in the " The main focus of the text is however provided by the Mumtaz Mahal's upper cenotaph. The angels recite the Quranic prayer, asking Allah to grant the faithful access to paradise. This is a touching request to God for His mercy towards Mumtaz Mahal, His servant devout.

Taj Mahal Impressions

It is a sight that anyone who walks by it cannot help but feel the urge to stop and look at it again. Its glory is something that anyone who has ever been there can't help but praise. It's inevitable! The Taj Mahal impressions are the thoughts and feelings people have after seeing this magnificent monument.

The impressions of Taj Mahal capture every emotion possible, from awe to amazement to pure ecstasy. These are just a few of the famous statements people have made about the Taj Mahal. These impressions were created by the stupendous beauty and pure brilliance that the monument displays. These impressions will leave even the most seasoned of people speechless.

Famous Sayings Of Taj Mahal

"The sight of this mansion causes sorrowful sighs, and makes sun and Moon shed tears. This world, this edifice was built to show, thereby the Creator's glory." Shah Jahan.

It looks like a flawless pearl on an azure background. It is a sensation I've never seen in any other work of art." Hodges, British painter

"I can't tell you what I think. "I don't know how to critique such a building.

I know what I feel. "I would die tomorrow to have so another over me." British officer Colonel Sleeman's wife

"Did you ever create a castle in the Air?" Here's one that has been brought to the ground and is ready for the wonders of the ages. Bayard Taylor, an American novelist

"I would not have done anything else in India if I didn't write my name here. The letters are a living delight."

Lord Curzon, British Governor-General

"You are aware of Shah Jahan. Life and youth, wealth, and glory all fade away in the currents of time. Therefore, you strove to keep only the pain in your heart. Let the glory of ruby, pearl, and diamond fade away. Let this Taj Mahal teardrop shine spotlessly on the cheek of time forever and ever.

Rabindra Nath Tagore

"Not an architectural piece, as other buildings, but the proud passions a emperor's wife wrought in live stones." Sir Edwin Arnold, English Poet

"And now, adieu!" -Beautiful Taj - adieu! "In the far, far west I will rejoice that I gazed upon your beauty; and the memory of my remains will not close until the lowly tomb a English gentlewoman closes." Fanny Parkes, Welsh Travel Writer

Ida Pfeiffer: "Pertinently, the Sultan's memory has been more sustained by this building than his favorite because everyone who sees it would involuntarily wonder who made it?"

"I was astonished to hear its praises every time I visited India, and I knew that it was beautiful.

Rather exceeded than fell short on my expectations."
Anglican Bishop, Calcutta. Reginald Heber

"Mumtaz Mahal, radiant in her youth beauty... India's noble tribute for the grace of Indian womanhood – the Venus de Miloof the East," Principal of the Calcutta Art School. EB Havell

"A white marble terrace is home to an immaterial light shell, similar to the apartments of

The blessed, whose feet do not touch the ordinary ground"
Swiss Art Historical Luminary Heinrich Wolfflin

It is a massive structure of marble, completely unweighted, and perfectly rational, but also entirely decorative. This is possibly the greatest work of art.

The forming spirit of humanity has never produced more work."

German Philosopher, Count Hermann Keyserling

Taj Mahal Main Gateway

Height: 93 ft high
Period of Construction: 1632-1638

The main entrance to Taj Mahal's mausoleum is known as Darwaza-i-Rauza, or "gate to the mausoleum", by Ustad Ahmad Lahauri the architect. While Taj is certainly stunning from a distance, it's the childlike excitement to see it from a distance that elevates the anticipations. Just as one reaches the main gate, the magnificent view of Taj disappears. Only to reappear when one is standing in the doorway, which leads to the main mausoleum. If one dives into an abstract interpretation, which suggests that Taj is a transition from the outer world to the inner spiritual realm, the concept of Taj emerging from the shadows and gradually growing on you becomes even more admirable.

One of five major elements of this majestic monument is the main gateway to the Taj Mahal. The Taj gateway, decorated with Hindu motifs and extending to the middle of the structure's height, is a niche-shaped doorway that looks like an ogival arch. The main entrance of Taj Mahal is characterized by vertical symmetry. It is bordered by Arabic calligraphy, which is made of blackstone, and contains verses from Quran. The optical illusion of an optical illusion is at work here. The letters have been made larger so that they appear consistent from top to bottom. This was achieved by increasing the letters' size in a pre-calculated way as the distance from the eyes increased. Part of the gateway also features octagonal towers on the corners. They are supported by wide, open kiosks with domed tops. A heavy door with eight metals at its base is also included. It has knobs.

The pointed tip of this niche is decorated with an image of a white and red teardrop, which adds beauty to the gateway to the Taj. This frontal gateway served the main entrance when the gateway was being constructed. These motifs reflect a Hindu touch. The niche's sloping sides are decorated with vines, leaves, and entwined flowers, especially red lotus ones. These motifs were created by semi-precious stones that were inlaid into the marble. The main entrance has an archway that leads to a large chamber with an arched roof. Experts have not been able to unravel the mysteries of the many rooms within it. They have twisting, branching and side-branched hallways that appear to have been used for three centuries. The most memorable thing about the show is the spectacular view of Taj from the main entrance.

Taj Mahal Mosque

A building built on the west side of the Taj Mahal, a Mosque constructed of red sandstone, enhances the existing splendor. It serves two purposes. First, it was required by Muslim law that every mausoleum have a place for worship near it. Second, the mosque and the mirror image of the Mosque, a guesthouse, on the opposite side, provide perfect symmetry to the architecture of Taj Mahal. The mosque is used for prayer purposes and faces the direction to Mecca. It is believed that it was built by Isa Mohammad. One large portal, known as an Iwan, dominates the exterior. On either side are two smaller arches. The mosque's stunning visuals are made up of three marble-coated domes and four small kiosks with marble veneer on the domed tops.

The floor in the interiors is elegantly designed and made of a material which appears to be velvet-red in color. It is in the form of prayer mats (569 in total). The mosque's interiors are decorated with delicate calligraphy that cites Allah and quotes from scriptures. The main distinguishing feature of the mosque is its presence of Minbar and Mihrab. The Mihrab, an enclosed enclosure with indented edges that marks the direction of Mecca as well as the direction where Muslims pray or perform salat, is the Mihrab. Minbar is the place where the priest gives a speech. It is located to the right side of the Mihrab. It consists of three steps leading to a flat platform.

A small enclosed space in stone measuring 19 ft x 6.5 ft is also located there. This was used as a temporary burial place for Mumtaz Mahal's remains until they found a permanent resting place inside the mausoleum dedicated to her memory. This enclosure is found along the western border wall, which also houses the well. The exteriors of the cenotaphs, crypt, and mosque have pietra dura decorations that exude an extraordinary elegance. All over the mosque, the name of Allah and verses taken from the Holy Qur'an have been repeated. The pool at the mosque is used for ablution prior to the prayer. Percy Brown, a noted art historian, observed that the Taj "resembles a spirited sweep rather than the slow, laborious cutting of an axel".

Taj Mahal Night Tour

Timings: 8:30 PM – 12:30 AM

Fee: Rs 750 (Adult, Foreign)

Rs 510 (Adult, Indian)
Rs 500 (Child between 3 and 15 years, Foreign & Indian).

Children under 3 years old are eligible for free entry (Indians and Foreigners).

It doesn't matter what time of the day it is when you look at Taj; you know it's going to be an experience to remember and share. But looking at Taj on a silent night when the moon is at its full glow is a moment about which you won't be able to maintain silence at all, until you've literally stalked and recommended each and every person in your sight to go visit the magnificent Taj when the sun is down. That's when rays of the moon light up the entire monument and lend it a faint silvery glow. Taj Mahal looks so mesmerizing on a full moon night that you will not even notice how the night passed and the sun came to bathe it in shades of pink. Wait no longer to adore at the Taj Mahal gleaming like a polished diamond under the moonlit sky. Go through the information below and book your tickets.

Although until a few years back the night viewing of Taj Mahal wasn't allowed, but in 2004 the government lifted the 20 year long ban and allowed for an initial viewing for three months after which it was made permanent. It is now allowed for 5 nights in a month i.e. on the full moon night, two days before it and two days after it, except on Fridays or the month of Ramzan. The night viewing is opened for four hours from 8:30 PM to 12:30 AM, for maximum of 400 people per day divided into eight batches of 50 people for duration of 30 minutes only.

The tickets for the night viewing of the Taj Mahal can be purchased one day (24 hours) in advance of the date of night viewing from the booking counter located in the office of the Archeological Survey of India, Agra Circle, 22 The Mall, Agra, Uttar Pradesh in between 10:00 AM to 6:00 PM. The tickets can also be cancelled at the above location on the same date of viewing before 1 PM with cancellation charges of 25% per ticket. Tourists must reach at Shilpgram (near Eastern gate of Taj Mahal) half an hour before the scheduled time mentioned on their tickets for security checks.

Inside The Taj Mahal

As majestically dazzling as it looks from the main gateway, with the glorious view of the mosque and the guest house on the sides and the main mausoleum in the centre with four minarets standing proud at each corner, the insides of TAj Mahal are no less stunningly beautified either. Rather, the painstakingly designed and richly carved interiors brilliantly compliment the grandeur of the entire structure with subtleness. With basic elements in Persian, the large white marble structure that stands on the square plinth consists of a symmetrical building with an arch shaped doorway known as Iwan, which is adorned with exquisite calligraphy and is topped by a large dome and a finial. The angles of the tomb consist of semi-octagonal arched alcoves of equal size. Attached pilasters rising from the base of the tomb demark each of the porticos, on both the sides. The main chamber houses the false sarcophagi of Mumtaz Mahal and Shah Jahan; as the actual graves are located at a much lower level.

Moving ahead, all the elements, architecture, furniture, and decorations culminate together to create an eschatological house for Mumtaz Mahal, and that of Shah Jahan. Formed with black marble inlaid in white, the floor of the Taj is paved in a geometrical pattern consisting of octagonal stars alternating with cruciform shapes. One of the longest echoes of any building in the world can be heard in this perfectly designed hall of 24 feet to a side, with two tiers of eight radiating niches. The natural and beautiful flowers like tulips, irises, daffodils, and narcissus filled in opulent vases appear here in basic tripartite arrangement rather than individual flowering plants of the pishtaq halls outside. Another remarkable feature that surrounds the cenotaphs of Mumtaz Mahal and Shah Jahan in the central chamber is the intricately carved marble screen or jali and is a delight to look at. The semi precious stones forming twining vines, fruits, and flowers inlaid delicately form the rest of the surfaces.

The burial chamber is located right beneath the central chamber and consists of the actual graves of Mumtaz Mahal and Shah Jahan covered by two cenotaphs. And since the Muslim tradition forbids elaborate decoration of graves, these cenotaphs have different motifs in their decoration. The real cenotaph of Mumtaz Mahal has an almost undecorated platform and is engraved with passages from the Holy Quran, promising God's mercy and forgiveness. Also, the ninety nine beautiful names of Allah can be found as calligraphic inscriptions on the sides of the actual tomb of Mumtaz Mahal. The cenotaph of Shah Jahan that was added much later is bigger than the cenotaph of his wife and is more simplistically decorated than his cenotaph above. Although the same designs appear on the sides of the sarcophagus elements, they are smaller in size. Coming out of such elaborately designed structure as Taj is like coming out of an era that had gone by, an era that added to the world in more than one way, an era that has been kept alive by the wonder that is Taj Mahal.

Taj Mahal Rest House

The Taj Mahal Rest House, also referred to as Guest House, Naqqar Khana, Mihman Khana, or the Assembly Hall, is located on the eastern side of the Taj and is a replica of the Taj Mahal Mosque that lies exactly opposite, on the western side of the Taj Mahal. It is believed that the rest house was built to provide a "jawab", which translates to "answer", as it balances the architectural symmetry and harmony of the whole structure. Although it is an exact replica of the mosque, a surety that this structure was never used for prayer purposes comes from the fact that unlike the mosque, it doesn't host a Mihrab, an indented enclosure that indicates the direction of Mecca and the direction which the Muslims face to perform their prayers or salat, and Minbar, a three step to flat platform from where the priest delivers a speech.

The entire structure of the rest house bears many similarities to the mosque at the opposite end. Just like the mosque, it is made up of red sandstone with marble facing that provides a captivating contrast of colors, possesses one dominant portal known as the Iwan with one mini Iwan on either side of it, three marble coated domes surmounted by gilded finials and adorned with flower-topped pinnacles and traditional lotus design, and four little domed kiosks with marble veneer. The finial that we see today was installed in 1940 and is fourth in succession after a series of repairs and replacements. The first was replaced back in the year 1810 by Captain Joseph Taylor. And as it didn't serve as a mosque, the Quranic inscriptions that present in the mosque have here been replaced by floral designs and other decorative patterns done on white marble that infuse liveliness to the red sandstone background.

However, till date, there's a sense of ambiguity to what purpose the rest house served. Apart from accepted belief that it was built to provide a symmetrical balance to the proceedings, theories from experts differ from it being used to accommodate visitors for observing the death anniversaries of Mumtaz Mahal to it being used as a rest house for the pilgrims who came here on caravans. Some also believe that it was used as an assembly hall where devotees used to gather before prayer. Despite all the theories that are up and running, one thing is for certain that the sense of grandeur has certainly increased manifold by the symmetrical design and identical twins of outlying buildings, the rest house being one of them.

Taj Mahal Gardens

By Lakun.patra (Own work)
Style: Persian
Divided Into: Four Parts
Canals: Two (crossing in the centre)
Flowerbeds: Sixteen
Trees: Cyprus & Fruit Bearing

The garden that starts from the end of the main gateway and ends near the squared base of the mausoleum is an integral part of the Taj Mahal structure and is, undeniably, one of the major highlights of the visit for many. The garden that beautifies Taj comes from the Persian Timurid style of gardens, and is based on the concept of paradise garden' and was brought in by Babur. This garden, filled with flowers, fruits, birds, leaves, symmetry, and delicacy, served many functions along with portraying strong symbolic or abstract meanings about paradise. A paradise which, according to Islamic beliefs, consists of four rivers: one of water, one of milk, one of honey, and one of wine. And it is from this concept that Char Bagh of Taj Mahal originated. Also, the symbolism of the garden and its division are noted in the Islamic texts that describe paradise as a garden filled with abundant trees, flowers, and plants.

Out of the total area of 580 meter by 300 meter of the Taj complex, these gardens alone cover an area of 300 meter by 300 meter distance and are based on geometric arrangements of nature. No attempt was made to give them a "natural" look. Another architectural attribute that has been followed in the case of the entire monument, especially the gardens of the Taj Mahal of Agra, is the usage of number four and its multiples. Since four is considered the holiest number in Islam, all the arrangements of Charbagh Garden of Taj Mahal are based on four or its multiples. The entire garden is divided into four parts, with two marble canals studded with fountains crossing in the center. In each quarter portion, there are 16 flowerbeds that have been divided by stone-paved raised pathways. It is said that even each of the flowerbed was planted with 400 plants.

The trees of the Taj garden are either that of Cyprus (signifying death) or of the fruit bearing type (signifying life) and even they are arranged in a symmetrical pattern. Taj Mahal occupies the north-end corner of the garden, instead of being in the center. In fact, at the center of the garden, between the Taj and its gateway, is a raised marble lotus-tank with a cusped border, which reflects the Taj in its waters. The four walkways that are although identical are differentiated through their context. In fact, the symmetry with which the whole garden has been organized and laid out, can be clearly observed and experienced as one can get an unhindered view of the mausoleum from any spot. These aesthetically maintained gardens not only bring a natural sense to the proceedings, but also make for some great snap taking spots. Taj Mahotsav Agra

Location: Shilpgram, Near Taj Mahal, Agra
Time: February, Every year
Duration: 10 days, 18th February to 27th February
Organized by: Department of Tourism, Government of India
Significance: Celebrated to promote rich arts, crafts, culture, cuisine, dance and music of the state and country
Highlights: A procession taken out in the typical Mughal era style, food festival, performances by folk musicians and dancers, etc

Taj Mahotsav is being celebrated successfully since 1992 in Agra in the month of February for ten days, from 18th February to 27th February.
Organized by the Department of Tourism, Government of India, Taj Mahotsav is mainly dedicated to the promotion of country's rich art and craft, culture, cuisine, dance and music. In fact, it serves as an acknowledgment to the craftsmen as well as the exponents of art, music and cuisine from all over the country. A large number of Indian and foreign tourists coming to Agra join this festivity of multi facets. The venue of the festival of Taj Mahotsav is Shilpgram, which is a stone's throw away distance from Taj Mahal. The festival starts with a procession, including bejeweled elephants and camels, drum beaters, folk artists and master craftsmen. A major highlight of this festival is the availability of fabulous works of art and craft at the most authenticated prices that are not sky rocketed by high maintenance cost.

This procession is an effort to reconstruct the ones that were taken out during the time of the Mughals. The crafts that are displayed in the festival have immense variety as over 400 legendary artisans from different parts of the country get an opportunity to showcase their talent. The crafts include woodcarvings of Saharanpur, brass and other metal ware of Moradabad, handmade carpets of Badohi, blue pottery of Khurja, Chikan work of Lucknow, silk of Varanasi, pottery from Khurja, shawls and carpets from Kashmir/Gujarat, hand printing from Farrukhabad, wood/stone carvings from Tamil Nadu, bamboo/cane work from North East India, kantha stitch from West Bengal, and paper & mash work from South India. Additionally, visitors also get to witness some of the spectacular performances by artists from every nook and corner of the country. The folk dances are sure to engulf you in their charisma and keep you enthralled for a long time.

One of the major attractions of the Taj Mahal Mahotsav of Agra is the Food Festival, where you can get some of the oldest and the most typical delicacies from the interiors of Uttar Pradesh and rest of India like chole bhature, Indian samosa, poori sabji, gulab jamun, Lucknavi kebab, South Indian dosa, Amritsari naan, Hyderabadi biryani etc. Throughout the Mahotsav, the visitors can experience the richness of folk, classical music, and dances from various regions of the country in the way they were performed centuries ago. Moreover, it's got something for everyone in the family as when the adults are busy with the arts, crafts, and cultural shows, the children too can indulge themselves in delightful food and fun fair that forwards various rides including the splendid roller coaster or the smaller ones like merry-go-round or train rides. Coming February, come and be a part of the festivity and you're sure to go home with feelings that'll have nostalgia running in every vein of your body in the time to come. And if this doesn't do it, the spectacular visit to the Taj Mahal will definitely do the needful.

Taj Mahal: Water Devices at Taj Mahal

Water Devices at Taj Mahal

The Charbagh plan that was beautifully adopted by the architects of Taj who wanted to give it a heavenly aura, did this by successfully incorporating the water devices, water which was brought from the river Yamuna, into the system in such a way that the garden looks full of life even after three centuries. The lush green grass, the unabashed floral beauty, the ever growing trees, and the most stunning features of all: an elevated lotus pond in the centre of the garden that gives a pure reflection of the Taj Mahal is a mark of architectural wizardry being put into action to perfection by carefully orchestration and putting up of water devices at the Taj Mahal in a very systematical manner. The end result was the already gorgeous view of the Taj Mahal is further enhanced by a total of 24 fountains on all four sides of this lotus pond.

Purs (a rope and bucket pulled by bullocks) were used for drawing water from the river and from there the water was transferred to a huge storage tank. Again thirteen purs were used to pump the water from the tank. From this tank, the water was taken into another huge storage tank through an overhead water-channel. From this tank, water was again pumped through fourteen purs and finally filled into three supply tanks through another channel. The last one of the supply tanks had pipe mouths in its eastern wall. These pipes entered the Taj Mahal enclosure from underground, with one of them moving towards the mosque to supply the fountains in the tanks on the red sandstone plinth below the marble structure. Part of the present water supply still uses the tanks of the old aqueduct, which are filled from wells by electric pumps.

For the fountains in the north-south canal and the lotus pond and its canal, copper pipes were used. To ensure uniform and undiminished water pressure in the fountains, a copper pot was provided under each fountain pipe. The water supply came first into the pot only and from there, rose simultaneously in the fountains, which means that the fountains were controlled by the pressure in the pots rather than pressure in the pipes. The main supply of the water in these pots came through earthenware pipes, some of which were replaced with cast iron back in 1903. And as for irrigational purposes, except for the outlets at the two extreme ends, the whole of the garden is fed with water through interconnected canals. Except for the ramp, most of the water devices at Taj Mahal have stood the test of time and are still present there. And it's the presence of these very water devices that the physical beauty of the Taj has been taken to an ethereal level.

A Day at Taj Mahal

Many of you would have heard stories about Taj coming alive under the full moon sky as if descended right from some spiritual realm, and that is exactly the case, no doubt! But Taj Mahal is one paradisal beauty personified! That means, whether it's the soft pink color at the break of dawn or the fiery yellow color it reflects at the brink of dusk, it's a sight to behold and is well worth a standalone experience; not to be compared with the pristine white radiance with which it sparkles at night. What's more, while at night visitors are allowed only for half hour duration; they can take as much time as they want to adore the spectacular Taj, right from sunrise to sunset during the day. And there's so much to observe and marvel at that rest assured, even a whole day would seem to pass by in no time. Since there is no limit on the time you may spend at the Taj on a single visit, you may remain here the entire day and let your eyes soak the splendor of the Taj.

Still photography is allowed inside the premises for free, except for inside the main mausoleum. Video making is allowed up to a certain area for Rs 25 per video camera. However, professional video making or shooting inside the complex is strictly prohibited unless prior permission is taken from the office of Archeological Survey of India located at 22, Mall Road, Agra. Mobiles phones are allowed inside the complex but are to be kept in the switched off mode. Visitors are also advised to go through the list of Do's and Don'ts before entering the complex. Tourists can purchase the tickets from near the western and eastern gate, where they are available from sunrise to sunset or from the southern gate, where they are available from 8 AM to 5 PM.

Facilities like cloak room at all the three gates, drinking water at eastern and western gates, public restroom on both sides of the main entrance, and a video locker room inside the main entrance where visitors can safely keep their video camcorders after shooting are available. Agra is one of the most important centers for handicrafts, especially of marble inlay work. Visitors who're interested in some serious shopping or even souvenir buying can engage themselves in the nearby markets of the Taj complex or Shilphaat in Shilpgram located just 750 meters away from the eastern gate of Taj Mahal. Here, visitors can buy authentic wares at reasonable prices. The Taj complex even has a museum that is open from 10 AM to 5 PM, the ticket of which can be purchased at the museum or the booking counter. With all this in place, and most importantly, the stupendous view of the Taj Mahal in the vicinity, it'll be a day to remember. Come and spend the day at Taj Mahal! Taj Mahal Legends

When the sense of mystique rises, the immortality of anything reaches an all time high. The myths and legends associated with the Taj Mahal consist of all the stories that have been said about it, but have not been proven to be true. However, all these legends of the Taj Mahal of India have added to the curiosity and have built up an atmosphere of mystery that seems irresistible. The intriguing element involved in these mysteries and speculations regarding how much of it is true have been attracting more and more people from all over the world to this marvelous monument. Some of the main myths about the Taj Mahal, Agra are:

Italian Architect

The Taj Mahal of Agra that has been illuminating heavenly for the past three centuries and more, and attracting and inspiring millions of people from across the world. It was built up by the Mughal Emperor Shah Jahan, who wanted his beloved wife to be remembered by one and all, with help

Black Taj

The Taj Mahal of Agra is one fine example of how to plan and then successfully apply symmetry into the proceedings. Every inch of Taj Mahal is a breathing example of it, except for one thing: the cenotaph of Shah Jahan himself, which appears to be an afterthought

Demolition of Taj

For long Taj Mahal has been a monumental figure, contributing to the epical history of the country. Clothed with white marble and ornamented with precious and semi precious stones, for long has it raised the jealousy bar in the hearts of the malice ones

Asymmetric Taj

The beauty of the ever graceful and magnificent Taj Mahal has always had admirers watch and praise in awe, and the symmetry of it has always had the architects from world across speculate and contemplate as to how this could have been done on such

Mutilation

Among all the fascinating myths and legends that surround the existence of Taj Mahal, there is one in particular that is the most grotesque. This legend tells the tale of the craftsmen who, one day were marveling at the stunning creation they crafted out of their own hands,

Name Legend

Although its name has been in use for as long as one can remember, nobody quite knows how the name of this beautiful, one of the Seven Wonders of the World came to be Taj Mahal. The "Name of the Taj Mahal" myth states various theories as to how this monument

Sinking Taj

As long as there have been magical monuments, there have been mystical and mythical tales surrounding them like fog on a misty morning. And the Taj Mahal of Agra is no exception to it. So, what myth is it this time? It's the myth of the sinking Taj!

Taj A Palace

Raved as one fine example of Mughal architecture with a style that brought Persian, Islamic, and Indian architectural elements together into one place and merged them to form the ever wonderful Taj Mahal, it is believed that the monument is one of a kind

Taj A Temple

Shah Jahan, belonging to the lineage of the first Mughal Emperor Babur, built Taj Mahal back in 17th century in the loving memory of his wife Mumtaz Mahal. Since then, this epic monument of love has been impressing and luring millions from across the world.

Theft In Taj

It is believed that when Taj Mahal first saw the light of the day, the precious, semi precious, and other priceless decorative items it was adorned with, shone as if the stars themselves came down to bask it in a heavenly glory. As many as 28 kinds of rare stones.

The first set of graves is placed in the central chamber, surrounded by an intricately carved marble screen or jali, inside the main mausoleum. The second set of graves is placed in the lower chamber, which is right below the central chamber.

www.ingramcontent.com/pod-product-compliance
Lightning Source LLC
Chambersburg PA
CBHW020946160726
47993CB00007B/2963